# Interview Me

*the complete guide to employment*

This book is dedicated to the woman who forced me to be better even when I thought I could not be. I am truly grateful for the tough, and I do mean tough love.

Love you mommy. Darlene S. Whichard

# Contents

# Interview You

It has often been a habit of my students to start questions with the phrase, "When I get to the initial interview..." This is the first common mistake made by job seekers. The initial interview starts before you talk to or even meet anyone at your future place of employment. When starting the process, you must remember this, "The interview starts with you." There are a few simple questions that we must ask and answer for ourselves before we print the first resume. Those questions are as follows:

I.     What can I do?

II.    Out of those things, what am I good at?

III.   Do I enjoy it?

IV.   To what field does it directly apply?

V.    How much is it worth?

VI.   What can I do?

As job seekers, we often confuse the want to dos with the can dos, in doing this we are led off course. As a result, we often apply for jobs that we would like to do or we think we deserve rather than apply for jobs for which we are qualified. The answer to the question of "What can I do?" is simple, look at the things that you have done in the past. These things should include jobs, internships, volunteer work, education, and recreation. Yes, I said recreation.

Though it may be unorthodox, a person's recreational habits will relate to some fields of work. For example, if you are a gamer and you apply for a customer service position at a local Big Box store or game shop your recreation comes into play directly. When asked what we are capable of, we often tend to leave important tidbits of information out of our answers. We have all had jobs in the past where we had to undergo training before the position started; though we gain a large amount of skill and education from these trainings, we never think to place them onto the resume. Training, be it on the job or in a facility or institute should be placed on your profile.

Training by definition is the education, instruction, or discipline of a person or thing that is being trained. Note that the definition does not make mention of a specific place or type of education, instruction or discipline. Be mindful that knowing what you are capable of is very important when starting your job search. Do not be hasty and dismiss training or skills that may seem irrelevant because of the time spent taking the training or where it took place. Be mindful that some of the most important trainings are taught in a matter of hours, i.e. CPR/First Aid. In a matter of hours, someone can learn to save a life.

*What am I good at?*

We should all ask this question of ourselves at one point in our lives. Even though in life this question has no easy answer, in the workforce it is quite easy to define. In this case, you want to think about the situations in past employment when your talents were called upon to do certain jobs repeatedly. During a normal workday, everyone has his or her role. What was your role? What was your specialty? What tasks were you asked to do the most over anyone else?

The preceding questions will assist you in determining what you are good at. Now, don't get frustrated when you think back and start to think of numerous things you've done, it's very possible that you are good at more than one thing. Being good at more than one thing is not a death sentence; in fact, it will serve as an incentive for your perspective employer. From a business stand point it just makes sense to hire someone who can wear numerous hats rather than someone who wears just one.

*Do I enjoy it?*

It is all too common to hear stories about a person getting up one day and realizing that they hate their job and that going back the next day was not an option. I, like most of the working class, once found myself in a job that I hated and realized that quitting was one of the easiest decisions that I have ever made. You are more likely to leave a job that you do not like and a lot less likely to leave one that you love.

The truth is, if you work a job that you hate, it is easy for you to decide that you are not going in on any given day. It is also easy for you to get up one morning and decide not to go back at all, which unfortunately happens quite often. In these cases, the employee does not bother with calling to let the employer know he will not be coming in or give the standard two weeks' notice of resignation. I have seen it a million times, two weeks go by and in you come to pick up that last paycheck, no one expecting you, no call, no warning. A word to the wise, find employment in a field of work you enjoy or at least a field in which you are comfortable. This will help to ensure that you will be with the company for years to come.

*To what field does it directly apply?*

Not all industries will survive over the years. Though painful to hear, some of us will have to change professions. For others changing professions is a choice, one that is made due to a number of reasons. For those of us who are looking for a new job in a different field or a different position in a familiar field, the question to what field does it directly apply, will come in to play. This question asks simply, what are your transferable skills? What skills from past activities do you possess that can be placed into action in your new position? For example, if you are applying for a job that involves computer usage, and you have had past experience working as a cashier on a computerized cash machine then the general computer knowledge exists.

Consider that navigating through a computer is a skill that not everyone has and not everyone is capable of learning easily. When answering the question to what field does it directly apply, you allow yourself to get a look at employment in other fields as well as requirements for positions in which you thought you were not qualified. It will also tell you how effective you will be in your new position.

*How much is it worth?*

When looking for employment asking yourself what you are worth is the wrong way to go. What you should be asking is, what are my qualifications worth? If you type 40 plus words per minute there is a price tag for that, if you can create and fill a Microsoft Excel spreadsheet there is also a price tag for that, and if you are a people person there is a price tag for that as well.

Answering this question is a matter of researching what general compensation would be for the position in which you are applying. Employees already in that particular field would be a good place to start your research. The United States Census Bureau also has a wealth of information when seeking out salary information. Though in our current job market it is a common practice to place an hourly rate in the advertisement for an open position, this does not necessarily mean that the rate given is the general compensation for that position. It is a good business practice to aim low with a job advertisement. This allows for negotiation with the right candidate.

A number in print is not an end all be all. In many cases, the company will have more money to support the salary of a person they deem too valuable not to hire. Hiring managers have a number of different aspects of their job. One aspect to keep in mind is that they are looking to save the company money by hiring the best help for the lowest amount of money possible.

Hiring managers receive a maximum dollar amount they are allowed to pay any one employee or a group of employees and the hourly wage or yearly salary is left up to them. For example, the hiring department or manager may be given a forty-thousand dollar budget to hire one employee or a four-hundred thousand dollar budget to hire ten. In some cases, more with salaried positions, the hiring manager makes the decision to hire and a management board decides the salary or, a board gives a hiring department the budget and allows the department as a whole to hire based on need.

## The Resume

Now the fun begins. Now that you have done your self- evaluation, it is time to formulate your resume. When writing a resume there are a few key things to keep in mind, these things are as follows:

1.  List all education relevant to the field of work you are going into.
    a.  Schooling
    b.  Training (to include on the job training)
    c.  Workshops/seminars
    d.  Certifications
2.  Keep in mind that certifications such as CPR, First Aid, Microsoft Office, and other software certifications would be useful to any employer in virtually any field.
3.  Keep your work history limited to 7 years or four jobs (only if jobs are held for 1 ½ or more).
4.  Make sure all skills that are relevant to the position you are applying for are on your resume (CPR/First Aid Certifications, computer programs proficiency, any machinery trained on etc.)
5.  Spell check is your friend; use it frequently. I am serious. Use it. I beg you. This could make or break your job search.
6.  Try to limit your resume to as little space as possible. Hint: Not too many people like to

read pages and pages of information. Do not panic if your resume runs over to two pages; just be sure that if there is information on the second page that it fills that page up. Blank spaces are not your friend. If there is a host of blank space on the second page of your resume consolidate it.

Let us start with the basics of the resume writing process. We will start with your Section Headers. The section headers list the sections of the resume that contain certain information about you. A resume should be clear and to the point and should include as much information about your experience and education as possible. All hiring managers generally want to know the same things. Those things are as follows:

1. Who you are.
2. What you are looking for.
3. What you were taught.
4. What you can do.
5. Where you did it.
6. Length of time you did it.
7. What you specialize in.
8. Whom they can contact to verify.

Though you are probably thinking that numbers 3, 4, and 7 are the same things, they are not. In fact, they are very different and very specific pieces of information. What were you taught is an education based question and is answered with the education header. What can you do is a skill based question and is answered with both the experience and skills headers. What do you specialize in is an experience based question that focuses on finding your strengths in the workplace and is answered with the experience header.

To answer these questions you will have a list of headers on your resume that will look like the following:

1. Objective (What are you looking for?)
2. Education (What were you taught?)
3. Experience (What can you do? /Where did you do it? /how long did you do it?)
4. Skills (What do you specialize in?)
5. References (Who can I call to verify this?)

Though I never suggest placing references on a resume the reference header is generally placed at the end of a resume to point out that the employer has reached the end of the document. Be mindful that there are several headers to use in a resume. Different headers could take it in many different directions. These headers provide a medium of advertisement for other experiences that cannot be classified with the more common headers. Remember, the following headers are not a requirement for your resume, but may be necessary in some instances.

1. Summary of Qualifications
2. Volunteer Experience
3. Certifications
4. Licenses

The Summary of Qualifications header gives the employer a quick overview of what is to follow in the resume. It is in a sense a preface or introduction to the person named in the resume. The summary should include pertinent information that is located elsewhere in the resume and is directly related to the field of work you are seeking employment in. The summary of qualifications header is a tool used to give the reader a brief overview of the information you feel is most important.

The Volunteer Experience header is used to chronicle relevant volunteer experience. Though you are technically working when you are volunteering, in many cases volunteer experience won't count toward your overall work experience with regards to human resources guidelines because as a volunteer your duties are limited to few things. For example, a hospital cannot have a volunteer who is a Certified Nursing Assistant actually take on the duties of a Certified Nursing Assistant due to its insurance structure. This header works exceptionally well for a job seeker who is looking to move into a new field of work, but has only volunteer experience in the field that he has chosen to pursue.

Though a large amount of your Certifications will make their debut under the education header there are a few that would serve no purpose there. For example, your CPR/First Aid certifications only take a few hours to train and test for, so this will not show up in the education section. It is generally the best practice to list certifications that has taken less than one year to obtain under this header. The one exception to this rule is if you have only one or two certifications, this will make this section look relatively empty. In this instance, placing your certifications under the education header is permissible.

The Licenses header is self-explanatory. This header should only house professional licenses. In addition, all licenses under this header should be current and up to date. To be more specific, if your license is expired then you are unlicensed. Now that we have gotten that out of the way, let us get down to business. There are things in choice careers that you just cannot do without proper licensing. For example, would you want a surgeon without a license to operate on you? Of course not, that would be absurd. Licenses pertaining directly to the field of work you are pursuing should be listed under this header and only if the licenses are valid.

The questions mentioned alongside the headers in the preceding text will be answered on your resume if it is written correctly and it includes the correct information. In a resume, you are selling a product that is in high demand, "No matter what the economists say about our failing job market."

Now, let us think of a salesperson, for this purpose, let us say that you are a used car salesperson. Are you with me so far? Good. When someone walks onto the lot and says, "Hi. I need a car." Do you then say, "Well, I have a nice one here, but it has 190,000 miles on it and the transmission is slipping. Oh, and the previous owner didn't take very good care of it, but I think this will be the perfect car for you?" No, you want to point out those things that would rope the buyer in. Now, I am not in any way telling you to lie, I am merely saying, "Put your best foot forward."

You can mention that the car has a great paint job and no damage to the body. You can mention that it has just had a tune up and full detail. You could even mention that the factory stereo has been upgraded; these are all things that would attract a buyer. Therefore, in the job market it is simply this, you are the salesperson as well as the car, the employer is the buyer, and your resume is your sales pitch.

Now that you have an overall picture of what a resume should be in your mind, it is time to focus on what it looks like. Resumes are like clothing; they come in all different shapes, colors, and sizes. Yes, I did say shapes and colors.

You will find that some feel very adamant about leaving a lasting impression on the employer; though in most cases having a resume that is oddly shaped or colored is bad, this very situation is great for you. It gives you the opportunity to show the employer what a good resume should be. Just so we are clear, colors and shapes are a no-no. In my experience, I have seen resumes arrive via many different mediums such as, mini-disc, colored paper, photo paper, videodisc, and lined notebook paper. If you are looking for an actual job, these are not the ways to go. The key to a resume that stands out is formatting. When writing your resume, remember this, readers often divert their attention to the areas that are in bold typeface first.

As confusing as the following may sound, please keep this in mind, the more elaborate and dressed up the resume is, the less likely it is to catch the right attention from the employer, and when a resume is too simplistic, to an employer this describes a simple person with a simple history. Both of these types of resumes will work against you. It is your goal to make your resume easy to read, but you also want to include the technical terms specific to your field of work. This practice lets employers who have actually worked in the field for which they are hiring know that you are familiar with the technical aspect of your job, and that you are knowledgeable of the field as a whole. This practice would also allow a recruiter who has never worked in the field to ask questions and get an illustration of what you are capable of doing.

In many cases, recruiters have tests available to evaluate the knowledge of a prospective employee. With these tests at the companies' disposal, it allows them to hire recruiters that are inexperienced in the field for which they are hiring, but are experienced in human resources. Here are a few simple rules to follow when formatting your resume.

1. Name should always be the largest object on the page.
2. Items in bold text should be only the things you want noticed first.
3. Never place references on your resume.
4. Make sure grammar and spelling are correct.
5. Make sure items are listed from the most recent date.
6. Include all tasks you carried out at a job not just those in your job description.
7. Remember to include any second languages as skills.
8. Know and list correct title for your position.

9. Use bulleted sentence structure to list job description.
10. If the job has only lasted for a matter of weeks, do not list it unless it was an assignment with a temporary agency.
11. Use a universal word processing program. (Microsoft Word, Open Office, Corel Word Perfect)

Once you have compiled the information that will fall under the headers that best fits your experience the next task is to put it together. The structure of the resume should be based on the type of job for which you are applying. The headers on your resume should be listed by its importance to the reader. For example, a person applying for a position in the building trades should list the experience on their resume before the education because the hands on experience would be more important than the education. If the person was applying for a project management position it would be more appropriate for the education to be placed ahead of the experience since a degree is likely required for this position.

Never written a resume you say? Well, there is a very easy approach. On a sheet of writing paper, simply jot down all the information you intend to place in the experience header. Be sure to write the items in list format. Once complete, the body of the resume is complete. The length of the experience section, which should be done first, generally determines the length of the resume. The objective will be done last.

The objective should be a short sentence or a group of sentences that tells the reader exactly what the job seeker is looking for. The objective should be placed at the top of the resume following your personal information. Once the information is written, transfer the information to a word processing program. When writing a resume remember the most important parts are correct spelling and appropriate information. The last step in the process is the formatting. Any lines, fonts, font styles, columns, or bullets should be added in this final step. Never add a border to a resume as it has no purpose other than decoration.

Over the years, I have been asked repetitively, "Why can't I put my reference on my resume?" My response over the years has always been the same, "Because we're human." When given a puzzling look I follow with an explanation of what I meant by the statement. Because we are human, we tend to forget that others are human as well.

We may have the same resume for an extended amount of time and forget that a great relationship with someone has turned sour and his or her information is still on your resume. A professional reference may have retired, been fired or resigned from the company he or she is listed as a reference for. On the other hand, the most common, one of your references has changed their phone number and has not had the opportunity to update you.

Though I could think of a million reasons why you should not put references on your resume one stands out in particular, "You never know what someone is going to say about you." Waiting until references are requested gives you an opportunity to contact the person you are using as a reference to let them know who will be calling and to ask what they will say once called. Now that you have this information, I feel confident that you will be more than happy to end your resume with the reference header and the phrase "furnished upon request."

## The Search

Over the years, I have had a number of students tell me that there are no jobs available in their respective fields. On each occasion, I offered the student a wager, a work or wage wager so to speak. The offer was very simple, if I provided ten current leads for employment, the student would be my office assistant for one week without pay, if I could not. I would pay the student a week's wage without the obligation of work. To date I have yet to pay one of my students for office work.

One very important part of looking for a job is resources. The resources you use to find a job are the most useful part of the employment process because without a job lead, there is nowhere to send your resume, and if you cannot send a resume, you cannot be scheduled for an interview, you get where I am going with this. If you never get an interview, you will never need this book. We cannot have that, now can we?

One could go about searching for a job in today's job market several ways. Unfortunately, with today's advances in technology it seems everyone looks to the internet for job opportunities as if it is the Oracle of the job market. In the text to follow you will find several job search tactics I have found to be quite useful. For the purposes of outlining job search tactics, I will describe these tactics using two groups of people.

Large company people-are those who look for employment with organizations that offer rapid growth. The large company job seeker will have his successes with online applications, job boards, and job postings because most large corporations strictly prohibit phone calls and faxes in response to employment ads.

*Large & Small Company Job Seekers*

Large corporations often make it a policy that all applicants must apply online. This allows the company to screen the applicants by way of online employment application filtering programs. For example, XYZ Corporation is looking for an office manager with an associate's degree. The company programs the application filter to automatically reject all applications and resumes that do not include the keywords associated with the position, such as manager, associates, college, university, etc. For the large company person, the internet, job fairs, and networking are the best mediums to pursue employment.

Small company people are those who search for positions in a company where their achievements will stand out greatly. Generally, in a smaller company the impact of the employees shine through very quickly due to the small staff. Looking for a job opportunity with a smaller company is done a bit differently than with a large corporation due to the companies' lack of monetary resources. In many cases, you will find that smaller companies are more receptive of employees who have families and need specific working hours.

Many small companies also offer incentives to employees such as, employee of the month programs, customer service awards, company/family picnics, quarterly bonuses, and performance based raffles. For this type of job seeker the internet, networking, local newspapers, and in-person job searches work best. Moreover, the help wanted poster still exists, my advice, keep your eyes open.

Between the two styles of jobseekers, two things are constant. Networking serves the same purpose with both styles of job seeker. It is used to build relationships with other employed people who could shed light on an employment opportunity not known to the public or to get to know other job seekers and find out what is working and not working for them. The internet however is used in two different manners with the small and large company job seekers.

For the large company job seeker, as stated previously, the internet is used for job search and application purposes. For the small company job seeker the internet is used as a tool to draw out potential employment opportunities. For example, the internet could be used to map out a driving route for local doctors' offices if you are looking for a position in the allied health field or to provide information about a business for which you intend to apply.

Even though there is no actual online application process, a host of small companies will post current openings online and direct applicants to submit a resume via fax or email. On occasion, you will also find postings that will include an address for an applicant to come in and physically apply. In either case, the internet is a very useful tool although you should not use it excessively or exclusively.

*The Search Begins*

Now that you have a bit of direction, it is time to start the search for your new job. In the resources section you will find a few online job communities to assist in your search. This section is included solely to assist in getting your job search started and should not be your sole source for job leads.

The job communities listed will assist in searching for employment without the limitations of website specific job postings. Going to traditional websites such as CareerBuilder and Monster will limit your search due to job posting having to be posted by the employer. However, there are large employers that advertise only on their personal website. This is done to draw in employees who are interested specifically in that company. The sites we will cover in the references section will allow you to search positions that are advertised on job sites and on private websites.

*Interview Preparation*

In our everyday lives, we often find ways to express our individuality to others. Now that we are in search of employment, we want to tone down our expressive personalities and tone up our impressive personalities. Our expressive personalities should only be directed toward friends and family. Our impressive personalities should be put to the forefront for the purposes of standing out in the interviewing process.

Though unfortunate and morally wrong, in today's job market you are judged by things that have nothing to do with who you are as an employee. The world judges us by things such as, body art (tattoos), jewelry, clothing, speech, and even hairstyles. Though these practices are frowned upon, they are a part of our world. Here are a few key points to get your impressive personality to the forefront.

## Key Point One
Initial Contact

The thing to remember is that an important part of the job interview starts over the phone. With that said, let us start with the basics. Be mindful that in order to schedule an interview in most cases an employer will call to speak with you. Stage one of your preparations is to change your outgoing voicemail message to include your first and last name and basic greeting.

It is helpful to remember that not everyone likes the same music as you do, and that not everyone speaks the same jargon as you. In some cases opposite music tastes can be offensive to a caller when forced to listen to music they dislike when calling to schedule an interview. Music and derogatory language should be left out, and background noise should be minimized when recording the message. In addition, remember that when receiving documents via email, the first thing the employer will see is your email address. Remember to get this professional as well. This means keep all of the sexual and derogatory connotations out of the email address. In addition, when given the option to input a name to be shown on receipt, this should be your first and last name as well.

## Key Point Two
First Impression

You must keep in mind that searching for employment is a job within itself and that between the hours of nine and five you should be in job search mode. To do this you must prepare a place to conduct conversations or phone interviews with the employer. It could be a possible disaster to answer a call from an employer while in a heated debate with your significant other, when you are yelling at the children or when you are in a social setting. This could cause the employer to have a negative impression of you.

When speaking with an employer by phone the most important thing is the first impression. In many cases, the employer does a small behavioral interview to ensure that they have made a good decision when they decided to go forward with calling you. Eliminate any distractions and try not to put the employer on hold other than to get some place quiet.

## Key Point Three
Preparation

Always have access to your schedule and a list of jobs for which you have applied. It is all too often that an employer will call a job seeker and the person they are calling will be completely clueless as to whom they are talking to. Remember the companies you have applied to and the positions for which you have applied. It can be disastrous to ask an employer what position they are calling regarding. Bottom line, this is something you should already know. This will show the employer that you have a genuine interest in the company and that you are not applying just to receive a paycheck. The goal is to have and keep an unblemished impression on the employer. Having a noticeably organized job search will assist in doing that.

## Key Point Four
Be Thorough

Remember to get as much information about the person you are talking to and the position you have applied for as possible while on the phone. Be sure to get the address and time of the interview and the name of the person you will be interviewing with, the actual interview may not be with the person you are speaking to over the phone. Ask if there is an online application so that you can fill it out prior to coming in. This gives you room for error and enough time to gather information to place on the application so that no spaces are left blank.

After setting the appointment for the interview, the next task is to fill out the application. With changes in the application process, filling out the application can go a number of ways. With online applications, the scheduling of the interview normally follows the application process. In the office or online the application must be filled out completely. In some cases, the application is only completed after the job is offered.

One of the most common mistakes of filling out an application is leaving spaces on the page blank. If some of the things on the application do not apply to you then it is advisable to simply put does not apply or not applicable. Due to a large portion of Americans that do not like to write, and are impatient, we make it a practice to speed through the application process. This is not the best practice. Speeding through filling out an application will only insure that you make grammatical and informational errors.

Another common mistake made in the application process is the signature. You must remember there is a significant difference between a resume and an application. The application is a legal document and the resume is a profile of sorts. The resume is a non-binding document. It is used simply to tell a story. An application is a legal document that requires a signature to verify that all information transferred from your resume to the application is true to the best of your knowledge. It is used to validate the information on your resume legally. Ensure that the information on your application matches the information on your resume, this will be important. In most cases, an employer will have both your resume and application in front of them when interviewing you.

## Dress to Impress

Though some industries may require particular uniforms to do a particular job, standard interview attire stays the same. One common mistake made by job seekers is to wear the industry standard uniform to the interview as if to say, "I'm ready to work." Though this is a noble gesture, this is not appropriate. One of the many purposes of the interview is to stand out. Because standing out is such a major part of the interview, wearing proper attire to an interview where everyone else has on uniforms is vital.

Before deciding what to wear to an interview ask yourself this, what makes me any different from the other applicants interviewing for this job? The theory is that you are aiming to be an orange in a group of apples. If you are a nurse, looking for work and appear at a local job fair dressed in proper interview attire and everyone else shows up in scrubs you would surely stand out amongst the other job seekers.

Things such as jewelry, tattoos, piercings, and hair should not be how you are remembered. When making your preparations the evening before make sure that all piercings, other than the ear for women, are removed. Also, be sure that all tattoos are covered and out of plain sight. Hair should always be kept neat and clean. Artistic hairstyles are not appropriate for interviews, nor should they be worn in the workplace.

One of the first things that an employer will notice is your clothes. Before leaving your home for the interview, you should ask yourself what your clothes say about you. Appropriate attire will let the employer know that you actually care about the job for which you are applying. We know that before the handshake and initial verbal greeting the interviewer sees and evaluates the job seekers appearance. Because of this fact, we know that your appearance serves as your very first impression.

When picking the right arrangement of clothing for your job interview there are some things you must keep in mind. This is not a social meeting; this is not a meeting with an old friend or a date, this is an evaluation of a prospective employee. You must remember that what you are wearing will play as much an important role in the interview as your resume. The following will offer an outline of what to wear to an interview.

**Attire for women**
*Common colors for women include navy blue, slate blue, brown, black, dark gray, and medium gray.*

When choosing attire for interviews there are things that are to be kept in mind. Because the options for clothing in women's fashion are so infinite, color coordination is very important. Blouses, purses, shoes, and suits come in thousands of styles, so the word of the day when choosing your attire for the interview is conservative. When choosing a suit be sure that if you are not choosing a solid pattern that you choose one that looks solid at first glance. The idea is to choose a pattern that appears as subtle as possible.

Women have the option of choosing a pant or skirt suit for interviewing. The skirt suit should be worn in a more formal setting. A standard face-to-face office interview would sanction both of these options, skirt or pant. If choosing a skirt suit, length plays an important factor. A common misconception is that a skirt should be knee length. The most confusing thing about the knee length rule is that it leads the job seeker to assume that the rule refers to the skirt being knee length while standing. The correct rule to follow is simple; your skirt should cover your entire thigh while sitting.

When choosing a suit it is best to ensure that the suit is the correct fit before purchasing it. When doing this it is a good practice to sit down in the suit facing a mirror so that you will know firsthand what the interviewer will see from his side of the desk. Also, ensure that the skirt is not too tight fitting and that the slit is not placed in the front of the skirt. Tight fitting would refer to the skirt that takes an hour to put on and zip up. A rear, center slit for a knee length skirt or a side slit on a calf length skirt would be appropriate for the purposes of the interview. High slits are not appropriate for the interview setting.

The pantsuit can be worn in any interview situation, but is ideal for an interview that involves movement. For example, walking up and down steps, getting in and out of a car, touring a site or facility, or working interviews would be ideal for a pantsuit. If the pantsuit is your attire of choice, ensure that the pants are not tight fitting and are clean and ironed.

As fashion evolves, pantsuits have become more and more elaborate with designs located on the pant leg and jacket. This is not interview appropriate. Ensure that pants are full length and that when you sit the pants do not rise too far above the ankle. The blouse should be a color that is not over bearing and should coordinate with the color of your suit. Shoes should also match your suit. Shoes should be leather and should be clean and polished.

Though stylish and may seem like a good idea, long heeled stilettos are not appropriate for the interview setting. Jewelry should be worn in moderation and be limited to a wedding and/or engagement ring and earrings. Earrings should be small and conservative in appearance for the purposes of the interview solitaires are best. Makeup should also be worn in moderation. Makeup should be used for the purposes of covering blemishes, tattoos and uneven skin tones. It should not be used to attract attention. Hosiery should be without runs or tears, and should be transparent or a subtle color that matches your suit.

**Attire for men**

*Common colors for men include navy blue and dark gray.*

Choosing attire for men proves to be substantially easier with the choices being so limited. Although it is common to see, black is not an ideal color for interviewing. Black is, and will possibly always be considered a formal color. Men have the choice of wearing a two or three piece suit depending on which is more comfortable and affordable for them. Be mindful that the three-piece suit is the more formal of the two, so be careful fellas.

Though you are not required to have a suit that costs hundreds of dollars, getting one suit that is good quality rather than buying a few poor quality suits would work in your best interest. When preparing for an interview it is important to make sure your suit is cleaned and pressed and that all stitched on designer tags are removed. Also, ensure that the suit is a solid color or resembles a solid color at first glance.

When choosing a shirt and tie, make sure that they complement the suit and that the colors are not overbearing. All shirts worn under a blazer should be long sleeve Oxford style shirts. The long sleeve Oxford should be worn in all seasons. Be mindful that spending money on a few shirt and tie sets of different color and styles changes the look of a single suit. This will instantaneously change that one suit into many different suits. This helps if a second interview with the same interview is warranted.

Jewelry for men should be limited to a wedding band and a conservative watch. Earrings and other piercings are frowned upon for men. If wearing facial hair, it should be trimmed and clean. Hair should also be kept neat and clean. Shoes should be black or brown leather and kept polished and clean. Soles should be in good condition and not worn. Socks should complement the suit and should not be any higher than mid-calf.

*Pre-Interview*

Over the years, we have all been told what is standard in interviewing. We have been told that we should arrive at least fifteen minutes to a half an hour early for an interview. We were also told that gray and blue are standard interviewing colors. What you may not have been told is that too much of any one color is overkill. Too much blue or gray will bring about a dismal feeling to the interview, though subtle it is an area to avoid. We were told to look presentable. One of the things I have come to realize over the years is that the things we were taught about interviewing were left unexplained.

In my experience, it is all too often that things are overlooked when preparing for the interview. You were taught to have breakfast before you interview and you readily assume that you were taught this because it is the most important meal of the day. The part that is overlooked is that it would be an embarrassing ordeal to have your stomach making hunger sounds in an interviewer's office. Another point to take into consideration is that the job seeker should be in a place where he can brush his teeth after having breakfast. Remember, it is not advisable to pick up an omelet that has onion and garlic while in transit. In order to interview well you must acknowledge that an interview is competitive and if everyone is doing the exact same thing, no one can win the competition for the job.

We are going to take a different approach to the interviewing process. We are going to appeal to the humanity of the interviewer rather than put this person on a pedestal as someone who holds your fate in his or her hands. In doing this, you must remember that the employer needs you as much as you need them. In fact, the employer needs you much more then you need them. Imagine a CEO of any company trying to do the accounting, purchasing, accounts receivable, accounts payable, scheduling, consultations, sales, collections, and janitorial amongst other duties in an eight- hour period. So, keep this in mind, one person cannot do everything.

The following is a list of things to help you prepare for the interview.

Ensure that you have gotten plenty of sleep the evening before and that if needed you have had plenty of coffee the morning of the interview

1. Arrive 30 minutes early for interview.
2. Make sure you have a fully stocked briefcase or attaché to include the following:
   a) Pens
   b) Pencils
   c) Calculator
   d) Note Pad
   e) Resumes
   f) Reference Letters
   g) Breath mints
   h) Application copy sheet
   i) A single page with all information required for the application.
   j) High school/college transcripts
   k) Any certificates or certifications receive for relevant education.
3. Leave excuses at home. Be sure to check your attaché or briefcase twice.
4. Make sure you have the name of the person who will be interviewing you.
5. Have two forms of ID.
6. Be prepared to wait and be alert.

7. Give persons entering the building a greeting as they pass.
8. Have information on the company you are applying for on hand.

Remember that in addition to your qualifications, you are aiming to obtain the likeability vote from the employer. As a rule of thumb, I often tell my students to treat the job search process as if it were a job itself. Doing the preceding will prepare you for work by ensuring that you have become accustomed to waking up in the morning at a scheduled time and are prepared to work. As a common practice, employers will ask a prospective employee when they can start; your response should be, today. If you treat the job search as a job, you will already be in the habit of waking up in the morning, and will have already developed a routine that works for you.

I am sure that most of you as I have; have always been told by your parents that one of the rudest things you could do when talking to someone is yawn while they are talking. Though you may be completely interested in what they are saying the uncontrollable yawning from the lack of sleep the evening before may make the employer feel as though you believe they are boring. This is not the better of first impressions. Lack of sleep also makes you less alert. This will cause you to do things like ask the employer to repeat herself or miss questions that you are asked.

This will not earn you any likeability with the employer.

I have always believed that there is a balance in the world. You must keep in mind that at every company there is always one person the boss wishes he had never hired. In every company, there is always a late person. This person is normally the person who does just enough work to keep their job. Unfortunately, we all know one of these people. A former colleague of mine called them slackers. For the job seeker these people are an absolute necessity. In arriving to an interview 30 minutes early, quite a few things are certain to happen. First thing, it is almost a certainty that the slacker will show up late on the day of your interview. The boss will see this. Showing up this early also allows you to see the kind of people the company hires and in some cases talk to some of the employees. This also shows the obvious; punctuality.

The most important factor of showing up this early is that it allows you to apply to the humanity of the employer. You will find that a large amount of people will feel guilty about making someone wait. You will use this to your advantage. When you arrive at the interview, you would normally report to the front desk to alert the interviewer of your presence, this does not change.

After being alerted of your presence a few scenarios could play out. The job seeker before you could have called to cancel or may not have shown up. You are hoping for the latter. Another scenario could be that the interviewer may not be busy, come out, and take you in for the interview immediately. This does not work against you because you are still early. The interviewer could also be swamped with work and plan to halt their work to interview you. This outcome is most favorable.

It is also very common that when a person makes another person wait for long periods, they feel guilty and when a person feels guilty in some cases they feel as though they owe you something. So, what does this person owe you? It may be a little understanding about the two-month gap in your employment history. Maybe she may owe you a substitution of education for experience or the reverse of the two. It could be virtually anything, but in any case, you obtain these ex-factors simply by showing up extra early.

When you arrive this early and the employer comes out to greet you after you have been waiting a half an hour the entire greeting process changes and the advantage is then handed to you. When you have been waiting this long, the employer starts his greeting with an apology for keeping you waiting. What the employer has not realized is that he is apologizing for keeping you waiting when you were on time; it just seems as if they kept you waiting for a large amount of time because you were so early. Remember to inform the employer that there is no need to apologize for making you wait and that you just like to be punctual.

One of the things to be considered is that not all companies are the same. The application and interviewing process differs on a company-to-company basis. For example, a former video game store did not hold interviews at all. In order to become an employee the current staff had to vote you in. They based their hiring simply on likeability. The tools in your attaché should cover all foreseeable scenarios. Some companies require testing; this is where the pencil and calculator comes into play. When testing you want to be able to go back, erase, and correct mistakes. The notepad will be useful for the interview the interviewer section. This is where you will record all questions you ask the employer and their replies. This will also come in handy to record new information about the company, a next interview or better yet, your new start date and salary.

Though you have sent a resume, you want to make the employers' job as easy as possible so, when you enter the office reach into that attaché and hand them a resume. It is advisable to pop a breath mint in and dissolve before entering the building because once you enter you will be in close proximity of others. You do not want to smell like this mornings' breakfast, especially if you are an onion lover.

If the application needs to be completed before the interview, the application sheet will be needed. The application sheet is a generic employment application you can print from the internet. It is completed in full so that you can merely copy the information from the sheet to the job application given by your new employer. The other items in your attaché case will be used upon request.

When preparing for an interview you want to make sure all bases are covered before leaving home. This means pinpointing your own shortcomings. If you are one who forgets things frequently, you want to make sure that all things are done the evening before. This would include putting your attaché and directions in the car the evening before. The worst thing that you could bring to an interview is an excuse. Excuses are sure to turn an employer off for one simple reason; if you will come to an interview with excuses, you will come to work with the same.

## The Interview

*The Interview Phase I*

Your first task is to greet the employer, male or female. A firm handshake is important. A firm handshake, for some employers, lets the employer know that you are not afraid of confrontation and that you can hold your own in a leadership role. For others, it defines how confident you are in meeting new people, which is vital in some areas of work. When shaking the employers hand ensure that you are looking them in the eye. This is your first opportunity to show that you have a high level of confidence.

When entering the interviewers' office, be mindful that it is not your home. It is all too often that we take the phrase, "Make yourself comfortable" much too seriously. To avoid this, I like to use something called the mirror affect. This is when you visualize the interviewer mirroring the same body language as you. As a child, you are told not to slouch in your chairs and not to place your elbows on the dinner table. Those basic principles also work for the interview. The following is a simple list of actions to be avoided in an interview.

1. Do not slouch in your seat.
2. Do not repeatedly look at your watch.
3. Do not stare at the floor or ceiling.
4. Do not stare at your resume.

5. Do not crack your knuckles or joints.

In most cases, we remember to sit straight up initially, but at some point during the interview, we start to get comfortable and overly relaxed. We often start to slide down in our seats. This can be mistaken for disinterest in what the interviewer is saying. You have to remember that this is the face-to-face first impression and that this meeting is the one that matters the most. As we all know; unless the interviewer develops a sudden case of amnesia, we will never get an opportunity to make a first impression a second time.

Like some others, I have been in uncomfortable public situations. One of the things that I have often used as an exit was to look at my watch before my retreat as if to say, "Wow, look at the time, I'm in a bit of a hurry I have to go." It is not in your best interest to make the employer feel as if your time is more important than theirs is. In the interviewing process, you want to keep the playing field leveled. Though this rule may seem unimportant, it would surprise you to know what most employers notice about your posture.

Growing up, I was raised by very strict parents, when they were talking to me, they would get extremely upset when I would stare at the floor and be unresponsive. When I would interview interns from the local college, I would often see the same practices. This would always remind me of my teenage years when my parents would talk to me and I did not want to hear what they were saying. Paying attention is very important. Looking at the floor shows that the person in front of you is not quite as important as what is on the floor in front of you.

Our work experience should be something that we remember. It is time we have taken out of our lives, for some it is decades of our lives spent with one employer. Reading from your resume implies that you are not being completely forthcoming about your employment and education history. With an exception of exact dates, information on your resume should be committed to memory. When interviewing a prospective employee, it is common practice to inquire about dates of employment. Employment dates gives the employer an idea of how long the job seeker has been in their respective field.

In a class I once asked a student about what he did for a living before deciding to go to school, he replied, "I was a cook." When I asked him what he did on the job from day to day he replied, "I cooked." As employees who do the same tasks everyday it is common to oversimplify what you do because you are so accustomed to doing it. Employees often get so comfortable in their position that they forget how important the job they do actually is. The fact is if the job you do has no importance no one would pay you for it. The fact is a cook does a lot more than just cook. Cooks cover a host of things on the day to day such as, test food for doneness and/or freshness, weigh measure and mix foods according to recipes, regulate temperatures of cooking devices, and order or purchase ingredients based on portions to be served. Simply put, a cook's job is a lot more than just cooking things.

When entering the office you should never take a seat without the employer offering you one. This is a costly habit. I stated earlier that this is not your home; however, this office serves as a second home to the employer. It is where she spends eight or more hours of her day. Taking a seat without asking would be the equivalent of walking into someone's home and helping yourself to his or her favorite chair or walking into someone's kitchen and making a sandwich without being offered or asking. This is very rude, and as I stated before above all else you are going for the likeability vote.

Once offered a seat your first action should be to offer the interviewer your resume and whatever references you have. Though you are sure that the resume you sent landed the interest of the employer, you should always offer another resume anyway. Doing this shows that you are prepared for anything even the occasional lost resume and cover letter. This cuts out the possible uncomfortable silence that may arise while the interviewer is looking for your resume.

Now, with your resume in hand and you in office the interrogation begins. You often get nervous when it comes to interviewing questions simply because you wonder if the answer you give is the one the interviewer wants to hear. In the following section, I intend to clarify what the employer is really asking so that you can give the employer the answer they are looking for.

### The Interview Phase II

The following will provide techniques that will assist in answering twelve of the most difficult standard interviewing questions. The following section is in place to ensure the job seeker answers the interviewing questions correctly. Keep in mind that everyone is different and that your experiences are different. The answers to these questions will be different for everyone, with that in mind, the questions and answers to follow are for the purposes of reference only.

Actual question: Can you tell me little bit about yourself?

Translation: Can you verbally state what is on your resume?

When writing your resume, because of limited space there will be information that cannot be included. This is your opportunity to speak about those things you feel are important that you did not have room to include on your resume or things that you wish to elaborate. The employer does not want to know about your personal life. Our personal lives could possibly paint a picture for the employer that will taint their image of you. For example, sickness, death, family events, and emergencies are all authentic reasons to miss work, but to the employer they are excuses branching from hiring someone with a complicated personal life. Telling the interviewer that you have children is the equivalent of telling the interviewer that you have legitimate reasons to miss work. Though harsh this is the reality of the world we live in, and having a family is unfortunately a liability in the employment world.

Actual question: Explain this gap in your employment history.

Translation: What were you doing for money or what was important enough to take you away from work?

There are things that hiring managers love to see and hear from a prospective employee. One of those things is their future employees' seeking education. If you left work to return to school, that would definitely be something you would want to tell the employer. One of my mentors told me once that it is always a good business practice to hire people that are smarter then you. This is the practice of paying people to think for you. Companies thrive under this practice. This is why it is great for you, the future employee, to mention this when asked about gaps in your employment.

It is also smart to make sure you tread lightly with your words if you left a position for family issues. If you are leaving employment for family problems, note that this decision is more for the benefit of the employer than that of your own. When considering leaving employment for family issues it is often a case where the employee foresees having attendance issues in the future and would rather resign then to neglect their responsibilities at work.

Actual question: What are your greatest strengths?

Translation: What are you good at? In what areas do you shine through?

We often describe personal characteristics like loyalty, determination, honesty, reliability, and responsibility as being strengths. When answering this question you do not want to tell the employer things that he already expects you to be. You also do not want to tell the employer that you place things that you should already be morally, on such a high pedestal. Personal characteristics should be a part of you and not something that actually takes a lot of work to maintain.

When asked this question we should focus on the things that would make us good at the job for which we are interviewing. If you are a people person, this is classified as a strength because it is something that not everyone is expected to be or can be. Being a people person is something that takes work. Your answers to this question should be limited to the characteristics you possess that apply directly to the position for which you are applying.

Actual question: What is your greatest weakness?

Translation: What can you improve on? What makes you less than perfect?

Be mindful that this question is supposed to find your shortcomings. The biggest mistake a person can make is to say that they have no weaknesses. This is dishonest and will immediately lose your likeability vote with the interviewer. Instead, you will use what I like to call the, "I lose you win strategy." When answering this question you want to offer an answer that works in the employers' best interest and may not necessarily be in your best interest. For example, if you are one who works until the job is complete, this may work out great for the employer because his projects are always finished, but when you continuously miss family dinners because you are working late this will work against you. A weakness is simply something that works outside of your best interest.

Actual question: Why did you leave your last job?

Translation: Were you fired from your last job? What were the circumstances of your departure? Did you leave on good terms?

In a perfect world, I would have come up with a method to maneuver this question so that the outcome will work in your favor, but the only real way of getting around this question is not getting around it at all. If there is any question about the reason you left your last job, be honest. Honesty is always the best policy when you are going for the likeability vote. If there was an issue with an employer that may create a problem, two methods that I have found will lighten the blow of bad news. The first is sending the blow early so that you can sooth the infliction later with your winning personality. When asked to speak about yourself you can include in your work history review why you are not with that employer anymore, but be careful and choose your words carefully because if the reasoning is too damaging you can kiss the job goodbye.

The second is a tad more thorough and gives you a bit of foresight. If you have a friend or relative who is in a management position at any company, you could ask them to request a reference from your previous employers. There are also companies that will do this for a fee. This will tell you exactly what the former employer will say about you. Knowing what a former employer will or will not say in some cases may be vital to answering this question.

Actual question: Where do you see yourself in five years?

Translation: How soon will I have to spend money to place a hiring ad? Do you have goals? If so, do they involve you being here?

Over the years, this has been one of the more entertaining questions asked in mock interviews. Undoubtedly one of the funniest answers I have encountered and surprisingly one of the more popular was, "In five years I see myself with your job." Would you hire someone who plans to put you out of work? I am sure you would not, so stay away from that answer. A hiring manger wants to know if you have plans to be with the company for some time.

Hiring managers need to hire employees that will make them look good and save them money. They save money when they do not have to pay more money to place ads repeatedly to hire new people for the position that has been abandoned. You make them look good when you stay for years and your work is above satisfactory. So be sure you are interviewing with a company in which you plan to stay.

Actual question: How well do you work under pressure?

Translation: Will you panic if things got a little hectic?

In some cases, the person interviewing you may be your boss when you are hired. In this case, the interviewer wants to know that if things get out of hand, he is hiring someone who will attack the problem with him rather than shy away. It is best to remember that quite a many employers judge an employees' worth by how well they deal with unpleasant or complicated situations. This is exceptionally true for retail careers.

Actual question: Why should I hire you?

Translation: Why should I give you my money? What makes you any different from the last experienced applicant?

During years of teaching, I have seen this question push someone to the brink of tearing his or her hair out. To the job seeker, this seemingly unanswerable question haunts them each time they hear it. This question should be just another place where you show off your talents. As job seekers, we seek the approval of the interviewer when answering the question, "why should I hire you?"

If you have followed the tips in this book, you already have the approval or likeability, if you will, of the interviewer. Nothing is free, was what we were to believe, though not true, free items are very few. In these recessive times, we rejoice at things we are given at no cost. When the employer asks the question, why I should hire you, the response should be as if you are having a two-for-one sale. For example, if you apply for a position as an office assistant and one of your former jobs happened to be as a copy machine repairperson, the reason the interviewer should hire you is because of what you have to offer from your former job experience as a repairperson.

In addition to your skills and education as an office assistant, you can also repair the copy machine when it gets broken and avoid the company having to spend hundreds of dollars calling a repairperson. Not only does this save the company money but also they think they are getting this service free. They are not; they are simply paying you with an audience. Someone will mention seeing you fix the copy machine, amongst other tasks, in the next managers meeting when it comes time for promotions and pay raises. This is when the services you rendered, that the company assumed were free are covered. These unique talents are referred to as transferable skills.

This is the ability to take training, education and skills from other careers or schooling and apply it directly or indirectly to a future position.

Actual question: Why did you choose this company?

Translation: Are you here just for a paycheck?

If you are reading this book then you probably have searched for a job and have applied for many as well. The interviewer wants to know that they are not your last resort, and that other companies want you. One of your goals is to make the interviewer feel as if they hit the lottery when they hire you. To do this you must make it clear that you have chosen this company as much as this company has chosen you. This is where your knowledge of the company comes into play. You can speak about the amount of time the company has been in business. The longer the company has been in business the more likely it will be that they will continue doing business in the future, and as long as they are in business, you will have a job. You can also mention things like potential growth within the company or things about a training program that you have heard about.

If you have gotten wind of a tuition reimbursement program it is also okay to mention that as well, giving that many companies require you to be with the company for at least three months before you even become eligible. Consider that when mentioning this you are offering a guarantee that you will be there a number of years.

Actual question: Why did you choose this career?

Translation: What drives you to get up and come to work in the morning?

A career should be something that you choose very carefully. You must understand the difference between a job and a career. It is simply this; a career is something you love to do, and a job is something you have to do. The employer wants to know what excites you about the position. What will make you get up every morning and come to work?

Actual question: What are your long and short-term goals?

Translation: Are you going to be with the company in the years to come? Do you plan to improve yourself?

Hiring people that are smarter than you has been a method of mega-millionaires for many, many years. It worked for Bill Gates and Donald Trump and the same will work for other business owners and managers. If you plan to go back to school, this is a plus because you are gaining more knowledge to exploit. Always mention things to the interviewer that will benefit the company. Things such as education, training, and taking on other responsibilities within the company are exactly what the company is looking for.

Actual question: Do you have any questions for me?

Translation: Any last words? Is there anything I forgot or you want me to know?

Be mindful that this is your last time to impress. The term, "Any last words," is associated with a person meeting their demise, but not in this case. In this case, it is a chance at new life so to speak. Here you would include anything you might have left out in conversation earlier on. This is another occasion where you get show off what you know about the company. Most companies' list company history on their website in the "about us" section, but there is always something for which to inquire. Though the position exists in one city, you may not want to reside in that city five years in the future. If the company is national, you may want to inquire about transfers in the future. Avoid at all cost saying no when you are asked if you have any questions, this shows disinterest in the company.

## Interview Styles

*Behavioral Interview*

The structure of behavioral interviews builds on questions designed to identify personal characteristics. If you are familiar with the Myers-Briggs Indicator tests, this will be familiar territory for you. The Myers-Briggs Type Indicator is a questionnaire designed to gauge personal or psychological preferences in how people make decisions and view life. In essence, the Behavioral Interview is a miniaturized version of that assessment. The following questions and answers will assist in guiding you through this form of interview.

Actual question: Please describe a situation in which you were able to use persuasion to get someone to see things your way?

Translation: Are you a strong salesperson? Can you lead other employees?

This question is very simple in nature. The question asks if you are comfortable with sales. The question is designed to find out if you are a person that takes "no" for an answer. Sales and marketing are the fields this question generally targets, but it will occasionally appear in interviews for customer service positions as well. In answering this question, remember to try to relate the situation to the position in which you are applying. This question can also be used to measure your leadership capabilities. To answer this question on a leadership basis, simply mention a time when in a group or personal setting you influenced a person or group to do what you wanted.

Actual question: Can you give me an example of a time when you set a goal and were able to meet or achieve it?

Translation: Prove to me that if I give you a task that you will actually get it done.

The goal of this question is to inquire about a person's ability to set and meet personal and career goals just as it states. This also allows the interviewer to get an idea of how motivated, creative and focused the prospective employee is. In answering this question, you want to refer to a story that outlines goals that you have exceeded, preferably one that was difficult to achieve. Be sure to include steps taken to meet and exceed this goal.

Actual question: Please give me an example of a time when you used good judgment and logic when solving a problem.

Translation: Are you a good leader or are you a follower? If given more responsibility, could you make good, sound decisions?

Like everything else in life, companies have problems on a day-to-day basis. This question will evaluate if you are a leader with the ability to make a solid decision when necessary or if you are someone who requires direction. For example, in sales, giving a discount to a new customer is a judgment call and will essentially be up to the salesperson to decide. Being a leader in sales will require being able to make quick and efficient decision and will surely ensure a good turnout with this example. If the customer has a good credit rating, well-paying job, the discount would probably be a good idea. The idea here is to provide a scenario that illustrates a time when you made a decision on your own that worked out well for the employer.

Actual question: Can you tell me about a time when you had to go beyond the call of duty to get a job done?

Translation: How far are you willing to go to ensure you do a great job?

This question gives you the opportunity to put on your cape and show off that "S" on your chest. This question will evaluate your effectiveness, drive, and loyalty toward your work and the company. When answering this question, you want to illustrate a situation when you have gone outside of your realm of responsibilities to get a job done. For example, I worked for a school in Mesa, Arizona for some time and used the copier to print class materials, one day the copier was not operational and needed repair, and fortunately, I had experience troubleshooting this machine and spent an hour, and a perfectly good white oxford fixing this machine. Fixing that machine saved the school hundreds of dollars on a service call and ensured the other instructors had the materials they needed to teach their classes. Later on that day, the associate campus director came into my office and personally thanked me for my assistance in the matter. Funny thing is; I did not know the assistant director had come in and saw me underneath the copier.

Actual question: Can you give me an example of a time when you motivated others.

Translation: Are you a team player? Could you take charge of my crew if I caught the flu?

First things first, in order to motivate co-workers you have to be a team player. It would be difficult for a loner to motivate anyone but himself if the person is always alone. When answering this question, you want to refer to a time when you provided a boost in morale to other employees through humor, offering incentives, or just being an ear to frustrated co-workers or customers. For example, my co-workers knew that I was sort of a "stick in the mud," and would never dance, I promised to do a dance in the office if we reached our placement goals. Everyone was dying to see this horrendous occasion so the team met the placement numbers and I danced. "And no, you may not see the video."

*Case Interview*

The Case Interview is unique in nature. You will find this style exists in the corporate world and in positions requiring professional licensing such as doctors, lawyers, and accountants. The case interview evaluates the job seekers ability to manage workloads and make decisions. The case interview is exactly what it sounds like. Candidates are given scenarios and are responsible for finding solutions. An inquisitive candidate is expected; this is part of the interview and will be under scrutiny as well. It is encouraged to ask as many questions as possible. The more you know the better the solution you can develop.

Because this style of interview is not based on the normal question and answer format, the same strategy will not suffice. The following will be an example of what you will be facing.

ABC Corporation sells car alarm systems that come standard on USA Cars. Because of financial reasons, USA Cars has to cut down its production costs. One of the first things to be cut from the production budget is the USA Cars alarm system. USA Cars decided to go with a cheaper car alarm and made the alarm system ABC Corporation sells available as an upgrade.

You will be given scenarios similar to the USA Cars dilemma. The employer will expect you to ask questions about the company and ultimately provide an opinion of what you think the best option would be for the company or client. Prepare yourself for a brainstorming session; this is in essence what the case interview is. When participating in a case interview remember that you should be thinking like an employee of the company in which you are interviewing.

*Panel Interview*

This interview I have lovingly coined the firing squad. This interview is given by a group of people, generally a board of some sort who collectively make a decision to hire. This interview is generally used to hire for corporate operations and other high salary positions. The idea behind this style of interview is to garner the opinions of other minds and to give a full spectrum interview. It is more likely that no questions will go unasked if there are four people asking them. This interview also saves the employer money seeing as this is generally a one-interview process. There are no second chances here. However, this like any other interview can be conquered; it is simply a matter of answering exactly what you are asked and no more. The questions in this style of interview will not differ much from the questions listed previously in this book; the difference here is that the questions are fired at you from a number of directions.

*Group Interview*

This interview is just as it sounds. You as well as a group of your peers will be interviewed jointly in front of a panel of interviewers. These interviews are designed to weed out the faint of heart. Companies that offer this style of interview are generally looking for candidates that are not shy or bashful and have the ability to speak in front of large crowds of people. During this interview, you are generally asked to stand and introduce yourself. Please be sure to filter the information that you give. Be mindful that the information given by the person before you may not necessarily be a right fit for your presentation. Censor yourself and remember that no matter how relaxed the environment may be that this is still an interview.

Although the types of interviews described now sound easy, they require much practice. It is advisable for you to go over your interviewing techniques with someone. As with everything in life, the interviewing process gets easier the more you do it.

Do not assume that once you leave the office that the interview is over. You are interviewed and evaluated on a daily basis even after you get the job. Be mindful that getting the job will prove to be the easy part though it requires a large amount of work, but doing a good job is an ongoing job within itself.

## Post Interview

Once you have left the company, you want to get to work immediately on the behind the scenes work. The first task is to contact your references that you placed on the application. References can be a bit of a nuisance because neither you, nor the reference will ever know when the employer is going to call. Because your references are not guaranteed to answer the phone, you need to make sure you have at least two others on reserve. Ensure that the references you choose are professional and have great phone etiquette. The term, guilty by association comes into play here because you are often judged by the company you keep. In this case, try to limit your references to the professionals in your life.

The next task on the list is a ritual long forgotten by job seekers. With the advance of technology, the written thank you letter has become outdated. The thank you letter offers the employer a look into who you are as a person. Writing a thank you letter gives you an opportunity to give your personal opinion on what you thought about the interview, the person who interviewed you, and the company itself. One of your goals aside from gaining the likeability vote is to stay on the mind of the interviewer. You achieve this when the interviewer receives the thank you letter and has to file it with the rest of the documents received from you. It is in your best interest to send the letter nearing the end of the business day to ensure that you are the last person the employer is thinking about before they leave to head home. The proceeding will list the different types of thank you letters and their uses.

*General Letter.* In this letter, you want to stress the things in the interview that stood out in conversation. If the interviewer seemed impressed by something that appeared on your resume or something you said, reiterate that subject in the letter. In this letter, also mention your appreciation for taking the time out to spend with you during the interview. At the end of the interview, you were asked if you had any questions, this is a courtesy, and is something in which you should voice your appreciation for as well.

*Damage Control Letter.* The damage control letter should cover anything that took place in the interview that rose concerns with the interviewer. Education and criminal background are the most common issues that require damage control. In many cases an employment ad lists the required education for a particular position, but what you will not find listed in these ads are the substitutions for required education. In many cases, work experience can be substituted for education. The lack of secondary education sometimes will raise a red flag with the employer. This letter gives you an opportunity to revisit your work history and restate how it relates to the position for which you are applying. Though with some companies, having a felony will bar you from employment for legal reasons (bonding, insurance, security clearance, company/client agreements, etc.) it is not the same for all. If on the job application you are asked if you have a felony, you want to be honest. Additionally, be aware of local employment laws that bar asking this question prior to hiring. The damage control letter allows you to explain why you have the felony and why you will never get another one. Be careful and word this letter very well. It helps to have someone proof your letter before sending.

*Suitability Letter*: The purpose of the suitability letter is to focus on transferable skills. Job seekers who are looking to change fields of work often use this letter. The suitability letter bridges past work experience with the new industry of work you are looking to go into. Some employers' look for direct work experience in the field that you are interviewing for, but will sometimes accept experience from other fields of work that are relative to the field you want to change over to. For example, sales to customer service, web designer to graphic designer, homemaker to United States President, you get the idea. Though these fields are different in title and in most cases may fall under different industries, they share the same base principles and/or qualifications. This letter also opens up an opportunity to stress personal characteristics that you feel fit the position for which you are applying.

In all thank you letters, there is one vital piece of information that is universal. It is imperative that you remember to say, "thank you" in the letter, thus its title, Thank You letter.

In the past, I was often asked if it were ok to call the interviewer after the thank you letter if you have not heard from them. The appropriate question is when is it ok to call?

The thank you letter creates your first opening to call the employer. This call can be placed to ensure that the employer received the letter that you email, mailed, or faxed. Unfortunately for you there is only one other opportunity to contact the employer without being too pushy. Over the years, I have found that just the thank you letter was not enough. A second letter should be sent in lieu of a phone call if you have not heard from the employer in a 72-hour period following the delivery and receipt of the thank you letter. This letter is called a Letter of Continued Interest. In this letter you inform the employer that you are still interested in the position and why.

In this letter, you also inquire about the status of the position. As unfair as it may seem, most employers will not call you to let you know that they have hired someone else. The Letter of Continued Interest also gives the interviewer a reason to inform you of his or her decision to go with another candidate. If in fact you are awaiting a response from the employer it is in your best interest to leave an email address, this creates another way of contacting you without having to feel the guilt of telling you over the phone that you do not have the job. When you reach the post interview phase the best things you can possibly do is to be patient and positive.

*The Offer*

Okay, you have impressed the interviewer and you get the phone call offering you a position with the company. What is next? Now it is time to find out what you will be getting out of the deal for all of your hard work and preparation. Generally, when an employer calls to offer a position to a prospective employee the salary is mentioned. If the employer does not include the salary in a job offer, it is acceptable to ask. Though you may be tempted to say yes to the offer before the employer completes the first sentence, do not, this is where the negotiation begins.

Now that the employer has made an offer, it is time to decide to accept or decline. If the employer makes an offer that is not to your standards, negotiation begins simply by asking if the amount offered is firm. If the employer asks if the offer amount meets your expectations, do not be afraid to answer honestly, as this may be your chance to get a higher offer. This also shows that you know your worth. If the employer states that is the ceiling for the offer, then you may want to consider other options. Options meaning your pay package not meaning another job.

Job seekers often forget a valuable piece of the pay package when considering a position. They often focus on the dollar amount they are being paid rather than the big picture. For example, if another company is offering more money for the same position, chances are the benefits package is front loaded on the employee. This company however, may be offering a smaller dollar amount and free or low cost medical insurance and other incentives like 401k matching or accidental death at no charge, so therefore the job with the smaller dollar amount may actually pay more because there is less taken from your pay.

When considering a position you must remember that the benefits package falls under your pay package. To make an educated decision, figure in what you will be spending for your benefits between the companies you plan to work for, and then subtract that amount from your gross, this is the number for which you should base your decision. The following diagram will illustrate the theory behind the decision making process.

| Company | Beg. Hourly/End Hourly | Monthly Cost of Benefits | Remaining Monthly Salary |
|---|---|---|---|
| ABC Corporation | $18hr $2,880 | $120 | $17.25 $2,760 |
| XYZ Corporation | $20 hr. $3,200 | $480 | $17.00 $2,720 |

(Reflects a 40 hour work week) Numbers shown are not exacting. Should be used for reference only.)

In the above table, you will see how a job that pays a lower hourly rate may work in your advantage. These numbers were created as a visual tool to guide you in understanding how to calculate actual hourly wage before tax. Some companies minimize their payout for benefits by increasing the hourly rate offered so the bulk of the cost of medical insurance and other benefits transfer over to the employee. In this conversation, you also want to ask about employment evaluations, bonuses and commission if they apply. In addition, how they will affect your pay.

Your first evaluation with a company will by far be the most important. Most companies base salary increases and incentives on how well an employee performs. Performance will be based on punctuality, organization, quality of work, efficiency, and availability, amongst other things. Your job now is to find out what the employer will expect of you so that the first evaluation is a good one. Be sure that during this phone call or meeting that you jot down what the employer is saying. This will be a great reference later on.

So far, you have gotten the pay package, incentives, and bonuses out of the way, now it is time for the vital information. Where am I working? Though both you and the employer will know what position you have been hired for, it is now time to inquire about reporting location, what you will be doing, what your hours are, and most important, when you start? Make sure that you jot this information down to assist in your decision making process. Additionally, do not be bullied into making an immediate decision regarding your future.

Although in some cases, your job description will be clear-cut and straightforward like a cashier, customer service rep, or security guard, however, many are not. Some companies will purposely change the title of a position to broaden the umbrella of tasks they can assign to one position. Other companies have duties specific to the company and have to create a title just to fill the position. In any case, it is always a good idea to ask about your duties on a day-to- day basis so that you are clear on what your job actually is. For example, while working for a medical trades school in

Arizona my title was Placement Coordinator, I was responsible for making sure the graduates had jobs when they graduated, made sure they had externships, tracked hours, taught career development courses, wrote resumes, and a host of other things. Because of the amount of different tasks I had to perform in my position, I could no longer be referred to as a Job Developer or a Career Advisor as my previous employers labeled me.

In most large companies, the hiring process is done on a large scale and generally done at one central location often in the style of a job fair. Managers from other locations will meet in one place and conduct interviews to fill positions at their respective locations. Generally, the hiring manager will furnish information about the particular site they are responsible for, but there will always be those who may leave out that information. In this instance, asking about where you will be working will be crucial.

This type of hiring process often happens with hotel, restaurant or retail chains. Companies such as GameStop, Inc., Wal-Mart, and Comcast are amongst the many that hold job fair style interviewing events. For example, if a hotel chain were hiring for ten of its hotels it would host a job fair at one of its location to keep costs down. This saves the hotel money on advertising and venue. If you do not ask or are not told which location for which you are interviewing, you might show up to the location where you interviewed assuming that location is where you are working, as one of my students once did. Be mindful that none of the information gathered from the phone call or meeting is useful if you do not know where you are to report to work.

## First Day

Okay, you have spent the weekend celebrating and partying like there's no tomorrow, and if this job has as many hours as you would hope, there will be no tomorrow, for celebrating at least. It is the evening before the big day and it is time to prepare. Though you have no idea what you will be doing on your first day, there are things that you should have just in case. The following is a list of things a new hire should have on his first day.

1. Pens/Pencils
2. Highlighter
3. Note Pad
4. Social Security Card/Passport
5. Picture ID (State or Government Issued)
6. Lunch
7. Small calendar
8. Voided Check (Direct Deposit)
9. An extra pair of underwear (for the extremely nervous)

The first day will be the most important of them all; this day sets the pace for your tenure with the company. On your first day the employer will learn if you are a, "hit the ground running" employee or a, "train to do" employee. Both types of employee have its vicissitudes. These "ups and downs" depend solely on the company and the work environment you are working in. A company may have a specific trademark way of doing things and may require you to train for the position or it may be the same position that you held previously. In any case, what you learn about the company the first day will determine what type of employee you will be.

Day one should be spent mapping your surroundings. This includes, but is not limited to getting to know your co-workers, learning company procedures, creating a comfortable workspace, making a schedule of daily tasks, and going over expectations with your boss. In doing this you will set a pace for what you will be doing daily and have room to make changes that fit your style of work. By the end of day one, if you have written everything down, you will have a detailed list of the tasks that are mandatory on a daily basis, and you will know when you have time to do other things within the company that may not be a part of your job description.

Another vital part of the first day is your new hire paperwork. These documents are required for any employee working in the United States. As I mentioned earlier, a social security card or passport should be with you and will be needed to verify your identity although a work visa or green card will be required for non-citizens. This will ensure that you are paid and that you can legally work in the United States. In this packet, you will find your W-2 form, I-9 or eVerify form, health insurance application, life insurance application, direct deposit form, job application, criminal background check, child abuse check, and release of information form. These forms will vary according to company needs.

Remember that the first day on the job is the day that you are expected to make all of your mistakes. The first day is the day you are allowed to make these mistakes without ridicule or consequence, use it. Although it may seem relatively unimportant, this is the time to learn the neighborhood. Asking questions about the local shops and restaurants will give you good reason to spark up otherwise awkward first conversations with co-workers. Co-workers are good references for the unofficial rules and regulations that exist in every workplace.

Cultures differ from job to job, a companies' culture is adapted by the employees and are generally in line to make the job and the working atmosphere for the employees more comfortable. As time goes on your co-workers will give you a heads up about infractions to these unofficial rules so that you will not break them. For some companies, the first day for a new employee is just as exciting for the current employees. Some companies have certain rituals that others may not. For example, I started at a company that purchased lunch for all new employees at the worst restaurant in the neighborhood. Knowing that this restaurant has been known for causing frequent trips to the lavatory, they use the eatery as a hazing of sorts. Needless to say that I spent the first 4 hours after lunch making repeated trips to the bathroom. Good times.

*Workplace Etiquette*

For some, spending more time at work then at home is a reality, but you have to keep in mind that both work and home are two completely different places. Home is where you generally make the rules and on many occasions break the rules with no consequence. Work however, is a place where rules have already been set in place and you, as the employee cannot change them. Now, let us get the most common rules out of the way so that we may continue.

1. Be early for work. (15 minutes)
2. Do not take any days off within the first ninety (90) days
3. Only call in sick when absolutely necessary
4. Take only scheduled breaks
5. Return from lunch on time
6. Do not smoke in or near the workplace
7. Stay a full day (do not clock out before scheduled time)
8. If required, be in uniform when you start work

Over the years, I have learned quite a few valuable lessons that have made me a better employee. The biggest lesson that I have learned is that in the workplace there is always someone watching your performance. I have learned that the monitoring process starts with the initial interview and continues throughout your tenure at a company. For example, if you show up for an interview 30 minutes early and start showing up late for work frequently, soon after you are hired, it is an almost certainty that someone will mention it. If an employer schedules an employee to work first shift it is implied that the employee will actually be on the floor working at his start time. You should never arrive for work at the time you are to start working. If you do, you are late.

In some states, an employer has a 90-day grace period to terminate a person without reason. This does not apply if you work in an at-will state, most states are. This period is considered the "probationary period" or the "evaluation period." The company is given this time to evaluate the employee without fear of a lawsuit if the need to terminate this person arises.

Generally, during this time the employer will offer none of the benefits that are tied into the position. During this time, the employer wants to see that you are showing up for work on time, completing assignments, adhering to policy, and work well with the team, amongst other things. The purpose of this time is to ensure that you are the right person for the company before the employer starts paying into benefits for you. So, in short, calling out sick, taking long breaks, smoking in front of the building, and being out of uniform does not show the employer that they have made the correct decision when hiring you.

In the following section, I will discuss best practices and characteristics needed to be successful in the workplace as a new hire. As previously mentioned, the first day sets the tone for your tenure at the company, however, the first 90 days are crucial as this is the time the company uses to determine if you are a good fit. Being a good fit with an employer is not just being capable of doing the job. If that were true, an accounting firm would hire Akshay Venkatsh the 15-year-old Princeton graduate with a double major in Mathematics and Physics. Being 15, Venkatesh would have nothing in common with any of the other employees other than the job itself. How could this person fit into the company culture with no life experience? It is about doing the job well. That includes functionality, personality, and reliability.

*Relationships*

Building relationships in the workplace is vital to your survival at a company. Your relationships will help you move up the ladder in regards to training. Consider that you could very well learn something from everyone you know at your place of work. It's a given that someone who has worked for an employer for a large amount of time will know more about the position than you will. It is also a given that a friend would be more receptive to training a friend rather than training the annoying new hire.

*Innovation*

While running a production company in Philadelphia, I realized there was something that the interns I would hire were lacking. All of the interns were doing exactly what they learned and nothing more. When I realized this, I made it a practice to hire employees who were creative. Over time, I tried to hire employees that were not afraid to make a job or task their own. I learned that creativity breeds innovation. Remember that the employees are the engine behind any company and that they create faster and easier ways of getting things done increased production for any company shines a light on the employee that developed the process.

*Responsibility*

Consider that an employer is buying your time, and as bad as that sounds, it is true. An employer wants to know that you can effectively do the job in which you were hired. Remember; always get a job description so that you will know what your key responsibilities are. Knowing what is expected of you keeps you on task and ensures that your responsibilities at the end of the day are met. In addition, this allows you to take on tasks outside of your job description if you complete mandatory tasks first. Taking on tasks outside of your job description will allow you to get valuable cross training, and show management that you are more than eager to take on other responsibilities within the company. Can you say promotion?

*Motivation*

In the workplace, motivation is what separates the enterprising people from the slackers. The slacker is the employee who comes in every morning late or just on-time, takes long lunches, leaves work early, and takes cigarette breaks, but doesn't actually smoke. The go-getter is the employee who comes to work early as if it were their first day, takes on extra tasks when able, stays late when able, and has a good idea of where she wants to go within the company. Motivation speaks volumes about an employee's loyalty and overall feeling of the company. Simply put an unhappy employee will more than likely be a slacker, and a happy employee will be the motivated enterprising star.

*Flexibility*

Like most companies, sometimes things come up unexpectedly. In many cases unexpected events plays a key role in a company's growth. For example, if a neighborhood is hit by a terrible storm, and you happen to work for a local contractor, business will pick up suddenly without warning and the company will look for flexibility in its employees to cover the extra work. Flexibility also ties into taking on other responsibilities on the job. For example, its dress down day, the copier breaks down and you are familiar with this brand of copier, you retreat to the copy room during your break, fix the small problem, and then return to your duties. Sound familiar? Things such as this are noticed by the higher-ups, and will be whispered for days amongst the other employees.

The aforementioned factors for success in the workplace are universal. These factors, if put into practice will ensure that you have many successes in your career. Though every company is different, a great employee should have the same underlying qualities as listed above. Be mindful that putting these ideals into practice does not mean that you should not be yourself; the best strategy would be to put these into practice in your own way.

Now that we have laid the groundwork for building a great employer/employee relationship, let us talk about the basics. Maintaining a great relationship with your employer entails lots of work and sometimes, great sacrifices to what one is accustomed to doing. The following is a list of things that are to be regulated in the workplace.

1. Email
2. Eating
3. Music
4. Telephone
5. Cell phone
6. Conversation
7. Attire
8. Hygiene

*Email* - Email has been a problem for employers since its inception. Chain emails, personal emails, and emails that contain secure information have been costing employees their jobs for as long as I can remember. During my research over the years, I heard a story once that may shed some light directly on why email can be so damaging. An employee without thinking sent an email that was intended for his wife. The email read as follows:

"I cook, clean, sing, write, and I'm a good man, and you should jump on me when I walk through the door."

The employee sent the email not realizing that he was in the middle of sending an email to the Assistant

Director of the institute for which he was working. He did not open a new screen and sent the email to his boss. Though his boss never commented on it, he knew he had received and read the email. Bottom line, work email is just that, work email, if you need to stay in touch via email with persons outside of your place of work, keep a private email account available. If you choose this option insure that there is no policy barring accessing the website that carries your email account.

*Eating* – This is a touchy situation for employees that spend a large portion of the day at their desk. It is common to hear, "I have a lot to do, and the company can't afford to be without me for an hour, so I'll just eat my lunch at my desk." Though that statement may be true, it is illegal for a company to have an employee work an entire 8 hour shift with no break. Be mindful that some foods have a very strong odor and that it will carry and linger in the workplace.

To some, certain smells may be offensive. For example, one of my co-workers at a past employer constantly ate at his desk. On one very memorable day this employee brought in tuna for lunch, this was a mistake seeing as it made the woman he shared a desk with sick. The employee he shared a desk with got sick all over the desk. That day I learned pregnancy and tuna do not mix. You could imagine that this was his last desk lunch. Before deciding to have your lunch at your desk, remember that it may be disruptive to the business, employees, and patrons alike.

*Music* – If you are anything like me, I sometimes need a distraction from the people around me in order to concentrate on pressing issues. For me, that distraction is often music. In fact, I am currently listening to my favorite tunes as I am writing. Though music is a universal language and is enjoyed by many, it is not appropriate for the workplace. It is important to remember that not everyone enjoys the same music. For the purposes of the workplace, headphones should be worn. This will ensure that no one is disturbed. Be mindful, even if you wear earphones, there could be consequences as well. Consider that some employers do not allow headphones in the workplace. Besides, how would you hear your boss yelling at you about wearing headphones if you have headphones on? Be sure to check the companies' policy about music.

*Telephone* – Telephone etiquette is very important in the workplace for many reasons. When answering the phone at any company you are automatically considered a representative of the company and everything you say is taken as if the company itself has said it. There are a few factors to be considered when thinking about phone etiquette. When answering the phone your first priority is to offer your attention to the person on the phone. This does not mean that you should ignore your surroundings by any means. In fact, it is a juggling process. In many cases, you are responsible for the patrons in an office as well as the phones. Therefore, here are some things to remember.

1. Always give the appropriate company greeting when answering the company phone.
2. Use appropriate language when speaking to someone in the office or on the phone.
3. Place caller on hold if a conversation needs to take place that is inappropriate for the caller.
4. Never take or place personal phone calls.
5. Do not place any out-of-area phone calls without authorization.
6. Control your tone and voice volume.

Remember that there is always someone listening so you should always conduct yourself as if someone is listening to your conversation. The truth is; many companies give employees non-disclosure agreements. They are designed to allow companies to monitor incoming and outgoing phone calls legally.

*Cell phones* – As unfortunate as it seems cell phones have ended many careers. Most companies have and strictly enforce cell phone policies. In many cases, the use of a cell phone is cause for immediate termination. Cell phones are not appropriate for the workplace for a number of reasons. The first would be an issue of security for a company that handles sensitive materials. With the advances of technology, cell phones often come equipped with devices such as voice recorders, camcorders, music players, and digital cameras. Think about a company that has something to protect, let us say Coca-Cola. It would destroy the company if an employee were to smuggle out their recipe. This can be done with one or more of the features of a cell phone. Cell phones create a distraction for employees that could cause costly mistakes in the workplace such as accounting errors or typos on important documents. Cell phones also increase the amount of breaks an employee will take during the day.

An employee will step away from their workspace several times throughout the day to take personal phone calls not considering that each time they step away they are taking an unsanctioned break. Bottom line, cell phones should only be used on authorized breaks. They should also be placed on silent, not vibrate, in the workplace. If there is an emergency, consider receiving text messaging as an alternative. There is no law against reading a text message. Sending one on the other hand, is a different story.

*Conversation* – Though being social and pleasant is the foundation of a good employee, conversation should remain professional. I am not in any way saying that every conversation had at the workplace should be about work itself, I am simply saying that some conversations are better left for companions outside of the workplace. Professional simply means, "keep a G rating on your conversation."

*Attire* – In today's workforce, it is common for companies to enforce strict uniform policies on their employees. Advertising is the reason for such policies in most cases and in other cases, they are necessary for safety reasons. Although there are companies that do not carry a dress code, that does not mean that one does not exist. Unless specifically told to dress down for a position, you should always stick to professional attire.

Professional in this case differs a bit from how professional is define for the purposes of the interview. For example, khaki pants and a polo-style shirt could be considered professional for a day on the job, but would be considered being underdressed for the interview. Many companies, you will find has a number of dress down days throughout the year that are in place as an incentive for its employees. Be mindful that there is always someone watching and that even though it is dress down day there is still an expectancy of you wearing something appropriate for work. With that in mind, no nightclub gear on dress down day.

In life, every place you go has rules to ensure the safety of the patrons and employees. As simple as some rules may sound or appear they are in place for particular reasons that may not be clear. For example, a few years back I traveled to New York City by train for a meeting and had to spend some time in the train station to wait for my car. There was a sign that said, "Do Not Lean Bags Against Wall."

Now, at the time I saw no point for the sign and put my bag there anyway. Later as my meeting progressed, one of my prospective partners noticed a large off-white stain on my briefcase. It was dried paint. On further inspection, I noticed that the paint on my briefcase rubbed off onto my pants and I had dried paint there as well. When I returned to the train station that evening, I noticed that a paint crew had been painting the baseboards and posting the signs. This was my first adult lesson in the importance of continuing to following basic rules.

*Events*

If you are anything like me, you party hard when it is time to party and work hard when it's time to work, but what happens when your employer has a party? How much should I drink? What time should I show up? What time should I leave? Should I bring a date? There are many questions to be covered in this touchy subject, so I will touch on the most important and potentially the most damaging.

If you are buzzed you have drank too much alcohol and are at your max prior to the office party, it is not in your best interest to start the night out with a drink, remember, there is always someone watching. At holiday parties, there always seem to be at least one employee that comes into the party, heads straight for the bar and clings to the bar like Glad plastic wrap. After the employees' stint at the bar, they often make their way to the manager or owner and tell them in a drunken ramble that they have thrown a great party. It is all too often that this person does not last with the company for more than three months following the party.

When considering what time to show up at an office party, remember that most employers only purchase enough time with the venue to set-up, clean-up, eat, dance, and mingle. In most cases, the party runs for about four hours. On occasion, companies will distribute tickets to employees that RSVP to cut down costs on food and alcohol, so be sure to show up if you request tickets. It would be in good taste to show up on time or no more than an hour late. Simply put, time is money and each second that you are not there is money wasted.

If your goal were to be noticed on this day, it would be beneficial to show up early to volunteer your services before the party begins. There is always a need for an extra hand. Think about it, how many parties have you gone to where someone has forgotten the ice? That said, showing up early to offer an extra hand will not go unnoticed, especially when someone brings up the party at work.

Office romance was something that I touched on in earlier text and will need to revisit for the purposes of answering the question should I bring a date. We have all heard stories of someone going out to a wild party and waking up after a wild party next to someone they do not know. Well, imagine waking up next to someone at the office. Next to the secretary, accountant, janitor, or in one strange turn of events that I once heard, an employee waking up next to the bosses wife. This could cause an unheard of amount of friction in the workplace. Especially if this is someone you do not particularly want to have a relationship with. To avoid a situation such as this, I suggest bringing a date to a company event unless the event is for employees only. Bringing a date makes it less likely that you will drink too much or wake up next to the bosses' wife.

Before exiting any company party, I have made it my personal business to thank the boss for throwing the party and to inform him of the things that I enjoyed at the party. This lets the employer know that you appreciate their generosity. You should never tell the boss that the party was great if it was not. Remember that you were both at the same party and because of that fact; they will know that you were being insincere. For example, I once told an employer that the food at an anniversary party was excellent, he then responded, "Thank you son, but what food were you eating?" From that day, I only comment on what I actually enjoyed.

If you have survived your first day and the first Christmas party then I would say you are well on your way to a very prosperous career with your new company. This means we have reached the end of our journey and you are ready to conquer your career path.

Remember to be on time, work hard, do more than expected, and whatever you do, stay away from tuna and cracker lunches.

There are hosts of other events that are held with employers. Especially employers with a strong company culture. The following will discuss two more events you may want to tread lightly while participating. Although there are no official rulebooks on how to conduct yourself at company sponsored events, there are a few rules to live by.

1. Not everyone likes what you like
2. Religion matters
3. Allergies exist
4. Going overboard will get attention
5. Not participating will get attention

We are all different. This is a part of what makes companies so successful. Having the different people from different cultures, economical climates, and educational backgrounds allows a company to get many different points of view and many different options to solve problems. That said, not everyone has the same background, like or dislike the things that you do. It is wise to get a consensus on what is liked, what is safe and in what everyone can participate.

A few years ago, I spent a week in Baltimore facilitating some workshops for a school. I was ultimately invited to the 10-year anniversary party of the school. Me, not tying the ideas that I was in Baltimore where the price of seafood is probably cheaper than the price of chicken and that there would be food at the party together, went hungry, ready to eat, and with shellfish allergies. Being a free food kind of person, my intent was to taste everything. Needless to say, everything was shellfish. Maybe even the wine. I and one other poor employee had bread and salad the entire evening.

Although I was an unexpected guest, there was still an employee left out and could not completely join in the festivities. I could only speculate on how the employee felt toward the organizer at work the next day. Moral of the story, allergies exist and religion matters. As to not alienate anyone, check for this

when having events that involve food and drink. In a
workplace, a Jewish or Muslim employee may attend a
celebration; however, both are not allowed to eat
pork. In addition, the Jewish employee cannot eat
shellfish. These employees may even find it offensive
if they are served.

## Note to Ex-Offenders

As the product of an inner-city neighborhood, I continue to commit to providing opportunities to those who are in transition to a new and better life. For those of you that has reached these final pages with the intent to employ the tips given, I give you one of my most effective reintegration methods, the C.R.E.D.I.T. System. Use it well.

*C*redibility - the ability to inspire belief or trust

In a perfect world, a man convicted of a crime would pay his debt to society and upon release have his slate wiped clean. No one would judge him for the person he was in his past life. Unfortunately, a perfect world is not what we live in. Because of this fact, an ex-offender will have to spend a considerable amount of time rebuilding his credibility.

In order to do this he would need to align himself with credible people who can vouch for him, including, but is not limited to, local politicians and organizations. State Representatives, Senators, Congressman, and non-profit offices are great places to volunteer time and develop relationships. These relationships will count most when being considered for a position. Getting a stamp of approval from credible people is a great way to regain your own credibility.

*R*esilience - the ability to recover quickly from setbacks

One of the reasons employers are so reluctant to hire ex- offenders is because of their lack of resilience. Due to the lack of the ability to recover, many ex-offenders tend to go back to what they know. Many ex-offenders misconstrue quick recovery with quick fixes. For example, a former drug dealer will go back to selling drugs to recover quickly. Eventually they are caught and sent back to prison. This is a quick fix; it is not permanent and results in disaster.

For the sake of this example, let us say this person also has experience as an automobile mechanic. A quick recovery would be to do car repairs until a permanent position comes around. Being resilient tells the employer that the prospective employee will not go back to his former life when things get difficult. Be mindful that each time an employee has to leave a position for any reason it costs the employer money. Being re-arrested will cost the employer money to re-hire and train another employee.

*E*ligibility - entitled or qualified to do, be, or get something

A common issue that affects many ex-offenders is that they often do not know what is in their criminal history. This will cause an issue in your job search. There are charges that will bar applicants from certain positions. For example, a person with a rape or domestic abuse conviction would be barred from employment at most medical facilities, schools, and childcare centers. Someone with a burglary, robbery, or fraud would not be eligible for employment at many retail stores. Knowing your charges will give you a look into what you are able to do with your convictions.

**D**elivery - the action or manner in which somebody speaks to an audience

When talking to employers, delivery is everything. As with any job seeker the absence of vulgarities and using correct grammar are imperative. Although vital, delivery is not limited to speech. It is a packaged deal. Delivery is the appearance of you as a whole. That would include resume, attire, speech, voicemail greeting, email address content, and a host of other things that affect how the employer perceives you. It also includes leaving behind "prison comparisons." Never start statements with "When I was inside," or "When I was upstate." You want to deliver a message that simply says, "that part of my life is over, time to move on."

*I*ntent - something planned, or the purpose that accompanies a plan/showing great determination to do something.

An employer wants to know that if they hire you, that you have plans. Plans tell the employer that you are moving toward stability in life. Stability comes when you are moving in the right direction. Those plans should include the position and possible advancement within the company. This puts the employer at ease about spending money on training you.

An open book policy with an employer will provide a clean slate for the employee and could be beneficial when the time comes to get on the advancement path. For example, if the job seeker tells the employer that she is looking to one day take on a supervisory position and later asks about training, this not only tells the employer that you are serious about your goals, but it says that you keep your word. Bottom line, your intent should not be limited to obtaining a position.

*T*alent - an unusual natural ability to do something well, especially in artistic areas that can be developed by training.

What can you do for me? That is the question the employer is asking. Remember that everyone has his or her own unique set of skills. Each of us has something that we do exceptionally well. This is what you want to bring to the forefront. With that statement in mind, consider that looking for a job that matches your skills is just as important as the eligibility piece. In short, identify your talents and use them as your selling point.

If you have been in any correctional facility chances are you did something that played toward your talents. No one spends five years working in a correctional facility kitchen preparing meals for thousands of inmates and not learn a thing or two about cooking. Remember, all experience is just that, experience, it does not matter where it comes from.

## Comparing Job Search Sites

*Employment Root Sites*

1. Indeed (www.indeed.com)
2. Simply Hired (www.simplyhired.com)

Root sites are not your common job search websites. They are different because they operate more like a search engine than an actual "pay-to-post" website like Monster or CareerBuilder. Root sites search the web for job openings that fit your search criteria. It searches private sites that post job opportunities on their own webpages and compiles them in one place.

The sites ask two simple questions. What and where? If you are a nurse relocating to Atlanta, you would simply type your profession and preferred location and the site will pull job postings from hundreds of other sites where postings exist. Keep in mind hospitals and large medical centers post positions on their own websites to keep down costs as well as most large retailers.

*Pay-to-Post*

1. Monster
2. CareerBuilder

These sites are like real estate. Ad space is sold to employers as well as the services of the writers and marketers. These websites are a great resource; however, they are limited in function. Simply put, if the employer did not advertise on the site, you will not see the job posting. Think about it in these terms, one of the largest retailers in the country, Walmart, does not advertise on these sites, they advertise on their own. In instances such as these, roots site are the more sensible choice.

Well, it has been a pleasure. I sincerely hope that the tips outlined in this section were helpful and produce grand results in the search and advancement of your career.

Good Luck and happy hunting!

Made in the USA
Charleston, SC
06 June 2015